T _____

From _____

Other giftbooks in the same series by Helen Exley:
Bon Appétit ...   True Love ...
Missing You ...   To my Husband with Love
For a Good Friend   Mothers ...

Published simultaneously in 1996 by Exley Publications in Great Britain, and
Exley Giftbooks in the USA.
Copyright © Helen Exley 1996

12 11 10 9 8 7 6 5 4 3 2 1

Border illustrations by Juliette Clarke
Edited and pictures selected by Helen Exley

ISBN 1-85015-794-4

Designed by Pinpoint Design.
Picture research by Image Select, London.
Typeset by Delta, Watford.
Printed in Singapore

Exley Publications Ltd, 16 Chalk Hill, Watford, Herts. WD1 4BN.
Exley Giftbooks, 232 Madison Avenue, Suite 1206, NY 10016, USA.

BON VOYAGE!

QUOTATIONS SELECTED BY *Helen* EXLEY

EXLEY
NEW YORK • WATFORD, UK

Bon Voyage!

Go lightly, simply.
Too much seriousness clouds the soul.
Just go, and follow the flowing moment.
Try not to cling to any experience.
The depths of wonder open of themselves.

FREDERIC LEHRMAN

May the road rise with you and the wind be
ever at your back.

IRISH TOAST

The little Road says, Go;
The little House says, Stay;
And oh, it's bonny here at home,
But I must go away.

JOSEPHINE PRESTON PEABODY (1874-1922)

Till a voice, as bad as Conscience, rang
interminable changes
On one everlasting Whisper day and night
repeated – so:
"Something hidden. Go and find it.
Go and look behind the Ranges –
Something lost behind the Ranges.
Lost and waiting for you. Go!"

RUDYARD KIPLING (1865-1936),
FROM "THE EXPLORER"

Never a ship sails out of the bay
But carries my heart as a stowaway.

ROSELLE MONTGOMERY,
FROM "THE STOWAWAY"

GO, TRAVEL!

*W*hy do you stay here and live this mean
moiling life when a glorious existence is
possible for you? These same stars twinkle
over other fields than these.

HENRY DAVID THOREAU (1817-1862)

If you come to a fork in the road, take it.

YOGI BERRA

Most people think they have too many responsibilities to travel, especially in the way that appeals to their fantasies. The hungry spouse, children, job, mortgage, school, army or Mother needs them. This is bullshit, of course. Most people are simply too afraid to step out of the rut to do something they would like to do. Honest, folks; The world doesn't end when you decide to do what you want to do, it merely begins.

ED BURYN, FROM *"VAGABONDING IN EUROPE AND NORTH AFRICA"*

Four hoarse blasts of a ship's whistle still raise the hair on my neck and set my feet to tapping. The sound of a jet, an engine warming up, even the clopping of shod hooves on pavement brings on the ancient shudder, the dry mouth and vacant eye, the hot palms and the churn of stomach high up under the rib cage.

JOHN STEINBECK (1902-1968)

I am fevered with the sunset,
I am fretful with the bay,
For the wander-thirst is on me
And my soul is in Cathay.

RICHARD HOVEY,
FROM *"THE SEA GYPSY"*

Once more on my adventure brave and new.

ROBERT BROWNING (1812-1889),
FROM *"RABBI BEN EZRA"*

Afoot and light-hearted I take to the open road,
Healthy, free, the world before me,
The long brown path before me leading
   wherever I choose.
Henceforth I ask not good-fortune, I myself am
   good-fortune,
Henceforth I whimper no more, postpone no
   more, need nothing,
Done with indoor complaints, libraries,
   querulous criticisms,
Strong and content I travel the open road.

WALT WHITMAN (1819-1892),
FROM *"SONG OF THE OPEN ROAD"*

Of the gladdest moments in human life, methinks, is the departure upon a distant journey into unknown lands. Shaking off with one mighty effort the fetters of Habit, the leaden weight of Routine, the cloak of many Cares and the slavery of Home, man feels once more happy.

SIR RICHARD FRANCIS BURTON
(1821-1890)

The earth belongs to anyone who stops for a moment, gazes and goes on his way....

COLETTE (1873-1954)

The healthy wayfarer sitting beside the road scanning the horizon open before him, is he not the absolute master of the earth, the waters, and even the sky? What housedweller can vie with him in power and wealth? His estate has no limits, his empire no law. No word bends him toward the ground, for the bounty and beauty of the world are already his.

ISABELLE EBERHARDT, b.1933

A good traveller has no fixed plans and is not intent on arriving.

LAO TZU (570-490 B.C.)

A good traveller is one who does not know where he is going to, and a perfect traveller does not know where he came from.

LIN YUTANG (1895-1976)

He who would travel happily must travel light.

ANTOINE DE SAINT-EXUPERY (1900-1944), FROM *"WIND, SAND, AND STARS"*

Travel like Ghandi, with simple clothes, open eyes and an uncluttered mind.

RICK STEVES, b.1955, FROM *"EUROPE THROUGH THE BACK DOOR"*

Take only memories. Leave nothing but footprints.

CHIEF SEATTLE (1786-1866)

There is an expression – walking with beauty. And I believe that this endless search for beauty in surroundings, in people and one's personal life, is the headstone of travel.

JULIETTE DE BAIRACLI LEVY, FROM *"TRAVELER'S JOY"*

Give me the clear blue sky over my head, and the green turf beneath my feet, a winding road before me, and a three hours' march to dinner – and then to thinking! It is hard if I cannot start some game on these lone heaths. I laugh, I run, I leap, I sing for joy. From the point of yonder rolling cloud I plunge into my past being, and revel there, as the sun-burnt Indian plunges headlong into the wave that wafts him to his native shore… I begin to feel, think, and be myself again.

WILLIAM HAZLITT (1778-1830),
FROM "TABLE TALK"

To awaken quite alone in a strange town is one of the pleasantest sensations in the world. You are surrounded by adventure. You have no idea of what is in store for you, but you will, if you are wise and know the art of travel, let yourself go on the stream of the unknown.

FREYA STARK (1893-1993),
FROM *"BAGHDAD SKETCHES"*

Seeing new places, new faces, hearing new sounds, wakes me up, makes me feel alive, makes me realize how quickly we forget that there's a great big world out there waiting to be explored, that there's more than our own small space, that beyond the blue horizon lie excitement, freshness, discovery, new people, new languages, new cultures – the unknown.

LAUREN BACALL, b.1924,
FROM *"NOW"*

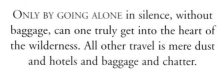

ONLY BY GOING ALONE in silence, without baggage, can one truly get into the heart of the wilderness. All other travel is mere dust and hotels and baggage and chatter.

JOHN MUIR (1838-1914)

The tourist who signs up for the round-the-world-in-eight-days jet lag special is left with bleary eyes and blurred memories. Yet the journeyer who immerses himself in a rain forest, clutches the side of a mountain, or punches the spray of a wild river discovers wells with unfathomed depths; windows overlooking infinity.

RICHARD BANGS, b.1950

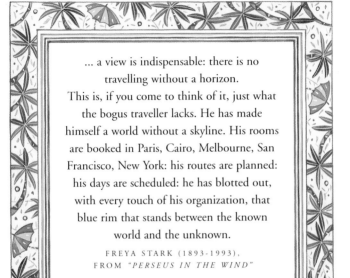

... a view is indispensable: there is no
travelling without a horizon.
This is, if you come to think of it, just what
the bogus traveller lacks. He has made
himself a world without a skyline. His rooms
are booked in Paris, Cairo, Melbourne, San
Francisco, New York: his routes are planned:
his days are scheduled: he has blotted out,
with every touch of his organization, that
blue rim that stands between the known
world and the unknown.

FREYA STARK (1893-1993),
FROM *"PERSEUS IN THE WIND"*

We have had an unspeakably delightful
journey, one of those journeys which seem to
divide one's life in two, by the new ideas they
suggest and the new views of interest they open.

GEORGE ELIOT (MARY ANN EVANS)
(1819-1880)

... travel is more than the seeing of sights; it
is a change that goes on, deep and
permanent, in the ideas of living.

MIRIAM BEARD, b.1901

Of all noxious animals, too, the most noxious is
a tourist.

ROBERT FRANCIS KILVERT

A tourist is a fellow who drives thousands of miles so
he can be photographed standing in front of his car.

EMILE GANEST

If you can commune with the mystery of past ages
elbow-to-elbow with a hundred camera-clicking
tourists – go for it.

PAM BROWN, b.1928

Guests at the Hilton Hotel are frequently reduced to
dialing room service to find out which country they
are in.

JOHN WELLS

There are tourists incapable of looking at a
masterpiece for its own sake. They bow into a
camera, snap experiences never had, then
rush home and develop these celluloid events
so as to see where they've been.

NED ROREM, FROM *"MUSIC FROM
INSIDE AND OUT"*

It began at first to dawn upon me slowly,
and was then forced upon me in a thunderclap,
that I had myself become one of those
uncivil travellers whom I so heartily
condemned....

ROBERT LOUIS STEVENSON (1850-1894)

The average tourist
spends more time lost
than found.

PAM BROWN,
b.1928

Travel is glamorous
only in retrospect.

PAUL THEROUX,
b.1941

The brochures do not always lie. A beach may be five minutes from the ocean. Free fall.

PAM BROWN, b.1928

The only aspect of our travels that is guaranteed to hold an audience is disaster.

MARTHA GELLHORN (b.1908), FROM
"TRAVELS WITH MYSELF AND ANOTHER"

It is only when you get home that you discover you were actually in the area, the street, the church that housed a city's greatest treasure.

PAM BROWN, b.1928

The only way to approach the Indian lavatory is in the spirit of the pioneers.

PAM BROWN, b.1928

HASSLES!

Thanks to the Interstate Highway System, it
is now possible to travel from coast to coast
without seeing anything.

CHARLES KURALT (b.1934)

You fly off to a strange land, eagerly abandoning
all the comforts of home, and then expend vast
quantities of time and money in a largely futile effort
to recapture the comforts that you wouldn't have
lost if you hadn't left home in the first place.

BILL BRYSON,
FROM *"NEITHER HERE NOR THERE"*

PHRASES HEARD FROM THE NATIVES: "It's never rained in May/June/July/August/September before."

"Last year this was a sea of wild flowers."

"When the mist lifts the view is quite stupendous."

"Chiuso (closed)." "This grotto is usually like the centre of an aquamarine." "They shut off the fountains last week." "Oh, that mural. Alas – last winter's floods…"

"I'm sorry. The picture is away on loan to the US."

"You've never heard of the Mistral?"

"I'm afraid that the entire area is closed – bombscare/archaeological excavation/new metro section/ visiting Head of State."

"They drained it."

PAM BROWN, b.1928

Travel changes people. It broadens perspectives and teaches new ways to measure quality of life. Many travelers toss aside their hometown blinders. Their prized souvenirs are the strands of different cultures they decide to knit into their own character.

RICK STEVES, FROM *"EUROPE THROUGH THE BACK DOOR"*

At its best, travel should challenge our preconceptions and most cherished views, cause us to rethink our assumptions, shake us a bit, make us broader-minded and more understanding.

ARTHUR FROMMER

FLYING? I've been to almost as many places as my luggage!

BOB HOPE, b.1903

Okay. You are somewhere, at least in theory, between Butte and Mobile, going faster than sound in a long metal container that is not in physical contact with anything. A slight jiggling sensation at your prostate (if you have one) is, essentially, all that is holding you up 30,000 feet above something that looks like a badly distressed suede jacket but is in fact the surface of the earth. You have been served a brown puddle with a lump in it, a rectangle of pale-yellow congealment, and some kind of mineral-based salad.

There is a wheeeeengneeeenngn noise. The jiggle-at-the-prostate feeling gives way to a kind of giving-way sensation. You are swallowed by a cloud....

ROY BLOUNT, JR., b.1941

Airline travel is hours of boredom interrupted by
moments of stark terror.

AL BOLISKA

I have never had any idea what goes on with other
people – but I have found that my major concern
in traveling in foreign parts is where is the ladies' room.
Now, in an airplane it always seems that it is as
far away from me as possible. And that the more
complicated and embarrassing the trip, the more
frequent my desire to make it.

KATHARINE HEPBURN, b.1909

… you define a good flight by negatives: you didn't get
highjacked, you didn't crash, you didn't throw up, you
weren't late, you weren't nauseated by the food. So you
are grateful.

PAUL THEROUX, b.1941,
FROM *"THE OLD PATAGONIAN EXPRESS"*

$\mathcal{F}$or some [travellers], there is simply the unashamed joy of staring at strange places, the pleasure of discovering what lies over the next hill and – most delightful of all – there is the fun and freedom of being alone, unhampered by family or phone, ready for whatever adventure may be on offer.

Such are the women, the loners, to whom travelling offers a means of giving rein to that contrary element of human nature which rises belligerently when roads appear impassable, when disinterested border officials shrug their shoulders and well-meaning friends advise against the whole impossible undertaking. Such travellers are adventurers.... They are society's square pegs: the guardians of our right to deviate, should we ever feel brave enough to do so.

MARY RUSSELL,
FROM *"THE BLESSINGS OF A GOOD THICK SKIRT"*

But there is one priceless thing that I brought back from my trip around the world, one that cost no money and on which I paid no customs duty: humility, a humility born from watching other peoples, other races, struggling bravely and hoping humbly for the simplest things in life.

FÉLIX MARTÍ-IBÁÑEZ,
FROM *"JOURNEY AROUND MYSELF"*

Travel is fatal to prejudice, bigotry, and narrow-mindedness, and many of our people need it sorely on these accounts. Broad, wholesome, charitable views of men and things cannot be acquired by vegetating in one little corner of the earth all one's lifetime.

MARK TWAIN (1835-1910)

I am not born for one corner; the whole world is
my native land.

SENECA (c.4 B.C.-c.65 A.D.)

Such delicate goods as justice, love and honour,
courtesy, and indeed all the things we care for,
are valid everywhere; but they are variously
moulded and often differently handled, and
sometimes nearly unrecognizable if you meet
them in a foreign land; and the art of learning
fundamental common values is perhaps the
greatest gain of travel to those who wish to live at
ease among their fellows.

FREYA STARK (1893-1993),
FROM "PERSEUS IN THE WIND"

Men and women [who] set themselves the challenge of going beyond the limits of everyday endurance... are in thrall to a driving force within them which pushes them onward – a force which they seem powerless to resist. The force has no name but its function is to explore the potential of the human species to adapt to conditions that are both challenging and dangerous. One could argue that a few individuals – sailors, fliers, travellers or mountaineers – while appearing needlessly to expose themselves to danger and death may, in fact, be unconsciously serving the interest of us all...

... standing apart from these reasons is the insatiable, intellectual need to know the unknown, to grasp the mercurial mystery of life itself.

MARY RUSSELL, FROM *"THE BLESSINGS OF A GOOD THICK SKIRT"*

The true call of the desert, of the mountains, or the sea, is their silence – free of the network of dead speech. This silence without which no enduring progress can be built must enter into all education that is worthy of the name: it is the reason why climbing or walking or sailing should come, if possible, into the life of every child.

Some people, out of strength or weakness, come to love such solitude as the breath of life. Many, strangers to their own souls, shun it with fear. But the well-strung creature finds in it a tonic, a pause from which he comes refreshed. With the mountain lightness still in his

eyes and feet, he is happy to return from the wilderness
and to find himself again among the paths and dwellings
and habits, the rites and symbols which in their long trail
of history have made him what he is.

FREYA STARK (1893-1993),
FROM *"PERSEUS IN THE WIND"*

That's the place to get to – nowhere. One wants
to wander away from the world's somewheres,
into our own nowhere.

D.H. LAWRENCE (1885-1930),
FROM *"WOMEN IN LOVE"*

To tell the truth there is something in the long, slow lift of the ship, and her long, slow slide forwards which makes my heart beat with joy. It is the motion of freedom. To feel her come up – then slide slowly forward, with the sound of the smashing of waters, is like the magic gallop of the sky, the magic gallop of elemental space. That long, slow, waveringly rhythmic rise and fall of the ship, with waters snorting as it were from her nostrils, oh, God, what a joy it is to the wild innermost soul. One is free at last – and lilting in a slow flight of the elements, winging outwards.

D.H. LAWRENCE (1885-1930), FROM *"SEA AND SARDINIA"*

As a traveler I can achieve a kind of high, a somewhat altered state of consciousness. I think it must be what athletes feel. I am transported out of myself, into another dimension in time and space. While the journey is on buses and across land, I begin another journey inside my head, a journey of memory and sensation, of past merging with present, of time growing insignificant.

MARY MORRIS,
FROM *"NOTHING TO DECLARE"*

The desert, like a powerful magnet, changes those who come within its field. Many travelers have felt it to be an almost mystical experience; others, a challenge to their humanity, to their very survivability. Some have found peace, some despair. Others have created from inner resources monuments of literature, philosophy, and religion. Perhaps the desert is no more than a magnifying lens, something that enables man to write large whatever he truly is.

WILLIAM R. POLK
AND WILLIAM J. MARES

He will carry, however faint, the imprint of
the desert, the brand which marks the nomad; and
he will have within him the yearning to return,
weak or insistent according to his nature.
For this cruel land can cast a spell which no
temperate clime can match.

WILFRED THESIGER, b.1910,
FROM "ARABIAN SANDS"

You will bring back pots and pictures.
A sheaf of photographs. A jingle of
coins. But you will bring back more.
A vision of a wide world.
Remembered laughter. New friends.
New understanding.

PAM BROWN, b.1928

How hard it is to escape from places!
However carefully one goes, they hold
you – you leave bits of yourself
fluttering on the fences – little rags and
shreds of your very life.

KATHERINE MANSFIELD (1888-1923)

… once you have traveled, the voyage never ends, but is played out over and over again in the quietest chambers… the mind can never break off from the journey.

PAT CONROY, b.1945

Travelling carries with it the curse of being at home everywhere and yet nowhere, for wherever one is some part of oneself remains on another continent.

MARGOT FONTEYN (1919-1991)

I think wherever you go becomes a part of you somehow.

ANITA DESAI,
FROM *"BAD TRIPS"*

The secret [of travel], indeed, is to have it behind you. It is not, like love or education, a process: it is like old china or glass, a collector's object, to acquire and possess.

FREYA STARK (1893-1993)

There is a second sort of traveller... who weave[s] in and out among the lives of people they encounter on the way, picking up, during their odyssey, a stitch here and a pattern there so that they return wearing cloaks embroidered with the rainbow of the world.

MARY RUSSELL,
FROM *"THE BLESSINGS OF A GOOD THICK SKIRT"*

Good days are to be gathered like sunshine in grapes, to be trodden and bottled into wine and kept for age to sip at ease beside his fire. If the traveller has vintaged well he need trouble to wander no longer; the ruby moments glow in his glass at will.

FREYA STARK (1893-1993),
FROM *"PERSEUS IN THE WIND"*

Beyond the East the sunrise, beyond
   the West the sea.
And East and West the wander-thirst that
   will not let me be.

GERALD GOULD, FROM "WANDER-THIRST"

A border is always a temptation.

LARRY MCMURTRY, b.1936

I cannot rest from travel; I will drink
Life to the lees…

ALFRED LORD TENNYSON (1809-1892),
FROM "ULYSSES"

For lust of knowing what should not be known,
We take the Golden Road to Samarkand.

JAMES ELROY FLECKER, FROM "HASSAN"

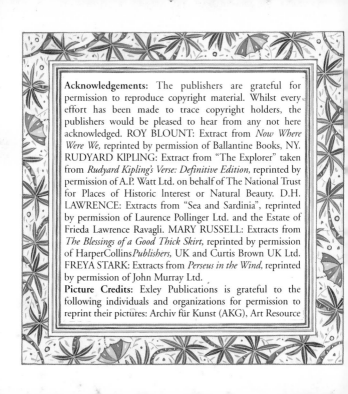

Acknowledgements: The publishers are grateful for permission to reproduce copyright material. Whilst every effort has been made to trace copyright holders, the publishers would be pleased to hear from any not here acknowledged. ROY BLOUNT: Extract from *Now Where Were We,* reprinted by permission of Ballantine Books, NY. RUDYARD KIPLING: Extract from "The Explorer" taken from *Rudyard Kipling's Verse: Definitive Edition,* reprinted by permission of A.P. Watt Ltd. on behalf of The National Trust for Places of Historic Interest or Natural Beauty. D.H. LAWRENCE: Extracts from "Sea and Sardinia", reprinted by permission of Laurence Pollinger Ltd. and the Estate of Frieda Lawrence Ravagli. MARY RUSSELL: Extracts from *The Blessings of a Good Thick Skirt,* reprinted by permission of HarperCollins*Publishers,* UK and Curtis Brown UK Ltd. FREYA STARK: Extracts from *Perseus in the Wind,* reprinted by permission of John Murray Ltd.
Picture Credits: Exley Publications is grateful to the following individuals and organizations for permission to reprint their pictures: Archiv für Kunst (AKG), Art Resource